BF Jones

the edge of nowhere

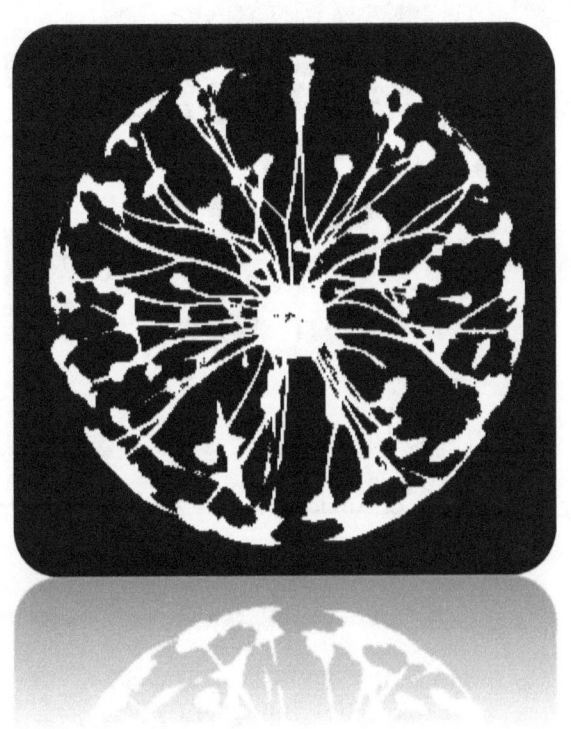

by
bf jones

Copyright © 2022 BF Jones

Cover by Cody Sexton of Anxiety Press & *A Thin Slice of Anxiety*
Interior design by Paige Johnson

www.Outcast-Press.com

(print) ISBN-13: 978-1-7379829-8-2
(e-book) ASIN: B0BQ64LPYV

This is a work of fiction. All characters, names, incidents, and dialogue, except for incidental references to public figures, historical events, businesses, and services are either products of the author's imagination or used in a fictitious manner not intended to refer to any living persons or to disparage any company's products or services.

"This is how we discuss

ourselves, and nurse desire

here as we gab about

the past, boneless as wool

dolls by a greenwood fire—

soon lit, and soon put out.."

~ François Villon

Grateful acknowledgement is made to these presses where some poems were first published:

Outcast Press Magazine, A Thin Slice of Anxiety, Punk Noir Magazine, Dead Fern Press, Pink Plastic House, Bristol Noir, Alien Buddha Press, Verse Zine, and Skyway Journal.

※※※

"Jones' terse style pounds the reader like a red-wine-headache, each poem a bitesize brutality—as opposed to a lengthy pity party—making for a perfectly impactful read." ~ HLR, author of *History of Present Complaint*

"B F Jones writes poems that are snatches of beauty and truth. Life and death. Taking everyday scenarios and embroidering them with shards of heart, soul and bone. Written in blood. B F Jones is one of the most wryly observant and honest poets writing today. You'll feel enlightened and contaminated, saved and damned, once you finish this collection." ~ Stephen J. Golds, author of *Half-Empty Doorways and Other Injuries*

"Visceral and fierce observations are exposed in dark poetry that's perfectly concentrated in each line and word. Jones paints very easily absorbed and unsettlingly relatable emotions. Powerfully crafted words and phrasing with such power and placement. Like the spirit of blues master gifting us a solo performance." ~ John Bowie, author of *Dead Birds and Sinking Ships* and the Viking Series

table of contents

The Anchor — Pg. 11

Window into the Drunken Soul — Pg.12

Landlord & Beef Jerky — Pg. 13

The Fall — Pg. 14

Beneath — Pg. 15

The Party Got Out of Hand — Pg. 16

3AM Drunk Text #1 — Pg. 17

Equinox — Pg. 18

Hungover #1 — Pg.20

When We Finally Meet — Pg. 21

On Catching Up w/ an Old Friend — Pg.22

On street Corners After the Office Party — Pg.24

Last Orders — Pg. 25

Date Night — Pg. 26

continued contents

The Best Scotch Egg in Town	Pg. 27
Skeletons	Pg. 28
Bad Move(s)	Pg. 30
Bloody Mary	Pg. 31
Do Not Resuscitate	Pg. 32
Wounds	Pg. 33
Feasting on Love Crumbs	Pg. 35
Ugly Thoughts	Pg. 37
Lies	Pg. 38
3AM Drunk Text #2	Pg. 39
Whiskey Head	Pg. 40
Russian Doll + Winter feat J. Travis Grundon	Pg. 41
Hungerover #2	Pg. 42
Time to Pretend	Pg. 43
Things I've seen & Things I Think I've Seen	Pg. 44

contents continued

Little Pain	Pg. 45
That Fight We Had Brewing	Pg. 46
3AM Drunk Text #3	Pg. 48
Remembrance Saturday	Pg. 49
Words	Pg. 50
Woman in Mirror + Little White Lies	Pg. 51
Vanishing	Pg. 52
Tombstones	Pg. 53
Wrestling The Beast	Pg. 54
Wreckage	Pg. 56
Toxic feat. Stephen J. Golds	Pg. 57
Last Words	Pg. 58
Bedtime Routine	Pg. 59
Repetitive feat. Stephen J. Golds	Pg. 60

continued contents

The Only Sounds Left	Pg. 62
Hide and Seek	Pg. 63
Queen of Hearts	Pg. 64
Trick or Treat	Pg. 65
Sleepwalking	Pg. 66
House of Cards	Pg. 68
The Conversations In My Head	Pg. 69
Memento	Pg. 70
Sang d'encre	Pg. 71
Attempted Ice Queen + Haiku For A Disappointing Man	Pg. 72
Every Time	Pg. 73
Un-love	Pg. 74
Summer Evening feat. David Cranmer	Pg. 75
Haikus to Nowhere	Pg. 76
Becoming Bark	Pg. 77
Unanswered	Pg. 78

last

orders

the anchor

It stands on the corner of the high street,
facing the chicken place,
the hardware store,
the tube station.

Rats sneak in
after last orders,
when the drunks spill out.
Some nights we can see them
scurrying about under the bar,
feasting on crumbs,
and discarded peanuts.
Agonising on poison,
distorted bodies
sleepy,
living carcasses.

Thankfully,
we are too drunk to care
and we carry on,
pretending they are not here,
pretending
none of that ugliness exists.

window into the drunken soul

Tony collects glass shards into the dustpan,
grumbles as he tapes cardboard
over the remnants of the window.

He keeps all the cardboard delivery boxes
for when the window gets broken
most Friday nights.

Last Friday someone almost died,
but today they are back.
They have a name,
but Tony doesn't want to know.

He empties the dustpan into the bin,
plasters the cut on his finger,
turns the lights off and
leaves by the back door.

landlord and beef jerky

William sits at the bar,
always at the same place,
on the same day, at the same time.
He sits where they used to sit,
he orders what they used to order:
a pint of Landlord
and a bag of beef jerky.

He drinks and thinks about what he no longer has
and what he will never do again.
He tastes memories
with every sip of the amber liquid,
hoping to retrieve her face
at the bottom of the glass.

He asks Tony to play "Feeling Good,"
a wedding song from many moons ago.
She'd tripped on her dress
and he'd caught her,
always caught her
until he no longer could.

the fall

It's not
an abrupt fall,
it's an inconspicuous one.
A slow descent, in installments,
one day at a time.
First,
you ignore it.
Everyone else does it,
right?
The morning afters are coffee,
sex and giggles.
Then you carry on,
though no-one else does.
The morning afters are self-loathing
and dry heaving.
You hide your venous nose under foundation
and your flask in your inside pocket.
Then you realise it's too late,
but it's too late.

beneath

She never said more than "Thank you"
for the drink he pushed across the bar:
lime and soda, no ice.
"This one is on me," he said on her fifth visit
and that's when they talked.
She talked.
Velvet draped in disquietude
and a half-smile.
"That's very kind of you. I'm Lucy."
Eyes suddenly latched onto his,
her destroyed soul springing out
from underneath her dark lashes,
a broken toy dangling on the end
of a rusty, distended spring.
He looked away from her dilated pupils,
scanning the rest of her:
turtleneck, long sleeves
on a sunny spring afternoon,
the remnant of a split lip
under bright-pink lipstick.
"Nice to meet you, Lucy," he said,
flashing his most impersonal smile,
quickly turning away
to empty an empty dishwasher,
dust perfectly polished tables
and wash the taste of his discomfort
with the last of her drink
after she disappeared into the night.

the party got out of hand

Someone has thrown up
all over the urinal
and someone is
passed out in the cubicle.
Someone is
sliding fingers
up someone
who is young enough
to be their daughter.
Someone has left
without paying
and someone has left
with someone else's husband.
Someone is calling 999
because someone has
fallen through the window.

Tony mops blood and vomit,
tapes the window,
turns the light off,
and leaves by the back door.

3am drunk text #1

I want

To lick your

Wounds

Clean

Start

Something impossible

Memories of

A broken

Love story

To take

To my grave

equinox

She's made effusive goodbyes
in keeping with the amount of alcohol she had.
She'd assured them that walking home was fine.
Fresh air will do me good.
It's fine.

A remnant of daylight still taints the sky.
Today is the longest day.
She walks quickly,
sways a bit, only a bit.

She didn't drink that much really:
three bottles of beer,
two large glasses of wine.

It takes more for her to feel it these days.
Alcohol is her lifestyle
and she's good at it.

There's a man walking ahead of her.
He might harass her.
Or rape her.
Or kill her.

Or he might be nice.
Might start a conversation.
Might befriend her.
Might take her out.
Might even love her

a little bit.

But he turns left,
disappears into a cab

and she's alone again.

hungover #1

She gets ready. Blouse. Earrings.
Shivers.
A thick layer of foundation. Lipstick.
Nausea.
Washed and brushed hair, loosely tied back.
Sweat.
She selects a backdrop conveying calm,
serenity, control.
The exact opposite of everything she feels:
fear, panic, desperation.

The six vodka-tonics from the night before
reappeared in the wee hours.
She spewed hot liquid and self-loathing,
punished herself with an ice-cold shower.
She forced down some scrambled eggs,
hating their texture against her teeth,
eroded by the acidic bile.

At 9am exactly, she turns her camera
and microphone on,
takes a deep breath,
smiles to the unfamiliar faces,
and starts talking.

when we finally meet

We sit at the bar,
and I say, "It's nice to
finally put a face on the name,"
and I laugh awkwardly
because I am awkward
and you are beautiful.

We drink too much
too quickly.
We talk too much
too quickly.
We kiss without
drawing breath.

You shut your mouth
with mine,
so as not to tell me
*I'm not the one
you were hoping for.*

on catching up w/ an old friend

They haven't seen each other in a while,
long enough to feel the need
to make small talk,
remind each other of their jobs,
their children's names and ages.

They count the years it has been
with tense fingers,
make dull conversation
that not even the wine
can lighten up.

Those evenings of inseparable fun
heady with weed and laughter,
unyielding with youth and hope,
are now a faint haze
from a different lifetime.

They try to reminisce,
but time has distorted their memories.
They don't remember the same parts
of that long-ago blur, and they can't
piece it back together.

They leave early and promise to catch up
soon.

But they know they won't.
The frail specter of their friendship
died there and then,
in between olives
and splashes of red wine.

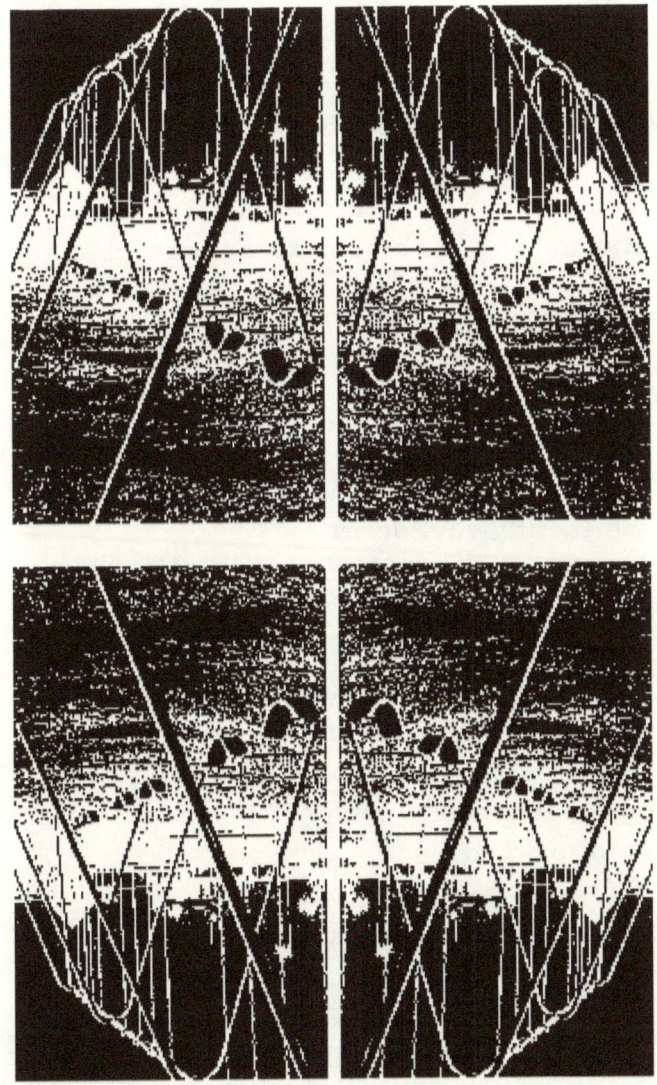

on street corners after the office party

You order a large cocktail in a bowl,
distribute straws around.

You all slurp the sweet turquoise liquid
and you feel her head next to yours.

You stand outside, smoking fags,
blaring out "Hotel California"
in-between two bouts of laughter.

Later, you kiss in a street corner,
whispering your desire
in corny 1970s porn terms and bad grammar,
sliding flies down,
sliding hands in.
You suggest a hotel, but she says no,
and unpeels herself from you.

I need to go home to my husband and kids.
And so do you.

She falls asleep in the cab,
and you stroke her hair.
In your head, love and hate
drunkenly punch each other.
In your throat, vomit rises.

last orders

The bell rings, church-like,
and they all flock to the bar
for that one last drink:
the one responsible for
ugly truths,
new friendships,
average dancing,
unsubtle snogging,
"Hey Jude" belting,
losing coats and jumpers,
regrettable text messaging,
tits flashing outside the kebab shop
in exchange for chips,
tears, laughter, love and fights,
vague memories
of a drowned youth
disappeared in the blink of a black eye.

date night

The band plays on a Sunday.
Same band,
same tunes,
same order.

They come every week
for cider blacks
and free live music.

They plunge their lips
in their first drink as
the band starts singing,
"Baby, it's a Wild World."

They drink their second
in tune with "Sunny Afternoon."

By the time
"Wish You Were Here" starts,
they're drunk
and glad that they are,
as he doesn't like
the song cover,
and she can't remember
the last time she liked him.

the best scotch egg in town

"I will take you to the place that has the best
Scotch egg in town,"
you say.
We squeeze past the crowds and get off the tube.
We emerge on the street, the icy air slaps our
faces
and you ask if I'm cold. I say no.
We haven't seen each other for months,
but we can't remember why.
We stop at Borough Market
and get served beers on a barrel.
We walk down the South Bank
and you grab my hand.
We sit on a bench and look at the river
And, finally, we kiss.
'Til long after the last Scotch egg has been served.
'Til way past closing time.
'Til the seed of heart ache is planted.

And we walk back to the station.
And I run for that last train.
And I look at your face shrinking into the night.
And my teeth start chattering.
And you're no longer here.

skeletons

They see I'm alone.
They think I'm lonely,
but I am not.
I like to sit here,
surrounded by strangers,
swallowed by a world
in which I don't need to act,
talk or make decisions.

I catch fragments of conversation,
they float around for a while,
dance with the steam
rising from my coffee cup,
wrestle with the echoes of music,
before they disappear.

Words with meaning or purpose,
words that might change a life.
"It's over," they say at table 7.
"12 weeks, almost 13," she cries at table 8.
"I like your tits," he growls at the bar.
"Can I get you a drink?" they enquire here and there.

"I like this song."
"Was he in Derek and the Dominos?"
"I'll have a Guinness."
"You're pretty."
"It's over."

"I'm bleeding."
"I miss her."
"Let's share a cab."
"Remember the stamps."
"Rex, sit. Good boy."

Words.

bad moves

He's on top of her,
breathing heavy
cigarette and stale beer
onto her scrunched-up face.

She shouldn't have picked him up,
but she wanted a distraction
on this moody, mundane evening,
and maybe some cheap fireworks.

She doesn't care for his white briefs
or his clunky, inconsequential moves.

He hasn't noticed
that she still had her shoes on
when he laid her on the couch
and immediately lifted her skirt.

He hasn't noticed the clenching of her jaw
as she despises herself —
as all she can think of is
the mud on her shoes,
the white briefs' distended waistband

and the man who once used to love her.

bloody mary

You've got to keep a brave face.
At least you can drink again.
You lift the glass to your lips:
Bloody Mary.

You savor the tartness
and the slap of chili.
You resist gulping it in one go,
put it back down on the coaster.
You catch the red drop sliding down
the glass with the tip of your finger,
wipe it on your napkin.

Around you, families are ordering
their Sunday roast, and, in the kitchen,
Yorkshire puddings pile up.
Hungry, happy faces all around,
fidgety children demanding straws
and a quid for the sweet machine.
The smell of gravy and
the rustling of newspapers,
the rays of winter sunlight
fading the already faded carpet,
and the crackling of fire in the chimney.

You take another sip,
and find the courage to smile.

do not resuscitate

The old guy comes in on Tuesdays.
He sits at the end of the bar, nearer to
the old-fashioned jukebox,
and orders a pinot grigio with ice.
He lifts the glass to his lips with a shaky hand,
looks around with washed-out, blue eyes,
and sometimes talks to Tony across the bar,
and Tony listens. He likes stories.

The old guy smiles at the past that he brings back,
his mind temporarily frolicking
in sprightly green grass.
He used to be an athlete,
and a scientist.
Now, he's an old man with a cane,
who sometimes forgets words,
who tries to buff memories
tarnished by age.

"Age is a shipwreck," he murmurs.
"If I start forgetting,
what do I live for?"

wounds

Beer
That time they said you were too ugly
to be their friend

Beer
And all the times after

Wine
That time they pinned you down and cut your hair

Wine
That time no-one picked you up at the airport

Tequila
All the times they didn't say, "I love you."

Gin
That time he slid his uninvited finger up you

Vodka
That time you were a body without a face

Champagne
That time you thought your life was finally
starting

Wine
That time his fist first met your jaw

Wine
And all the times after

Lime and soda
That time you decided to sort your life out.

feasting on love crumbs

Carla wears her favorite jeans to her date.
There is a very small stain on the right knee,
from when she'd been frying an egg,
and a drop of oil had escaped and landed there.

The burn had her recoil but was soon forgotten.

Only a miniature dot had scarred the denim,
and only she can see it
because she knows it's there.
She sometimes looks for it,
looks
and feels sorry.

He makes her feel so special,
admired,
desired.

So what, if he occasionally
says things she'd rather not hear?

She's so childish.
She has issues.
She's not worth him.
Shouldn't doubt him.

On her way home, she notices

a stain of ketchup on her sleeve,
a bloody smudge
that she tries to lick clean.

But it only fades

and never disappears.

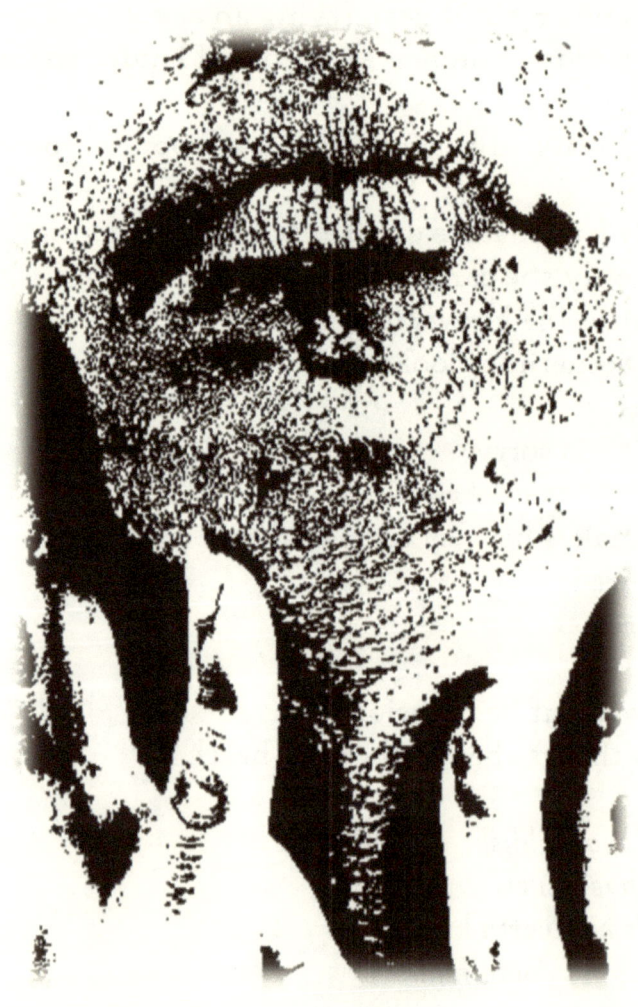

ugly thoughts

Let's drown them,
those bad thoughts,
like unwanted kittens
meowing with despair.

Let's pour amber liquid
over those coffins
and dance around those graves.
Let's play one more tune
before we pass out.

Let's weigh them down
with beer and rum
so that they don't resurface,
baring blatant decay
and the smell of no more.

Let's drown them.

lies

He doesn't exist.
He's just Uncle Jeff,
whose knee you sit on,
who is secretly enjoying
the contact of your young flesh.

There is no such thing
as spending all that time
with your tennis partner,
but it's so much easier
to believe.
Or that friendship,
cheap and impossibly shiny,
gold-sprayed rusty metal
rubbing away fast, leaving
blood-colored stains.

And all wounds don't heal with time.
Who the fuck said that?
They re-open unexpectedly,
tearing pink and fresh
under the claws of timeless betrayal.

3am drunk text #2

I want to shout

Your name.

I dry out

Lusty sweat

And wet fingers

And wonder if

You

And I

Will one day

Come

Together

whiskey head

The city in my mind
is disquieting and dark,
a shade of blood maroon
that turns my echoing footsteps
into a fearful cavalcade.

All streets are murderous corners.
All roads lead to nowhere
and hope clings to trees
that have long ceased to grow.

I'm a dead man walking,
following the sinuation
of a seamy river
that carries the anniversaries of
Unexplained deaths,
the remains of
Unclaimed bodies
and unloved souls.

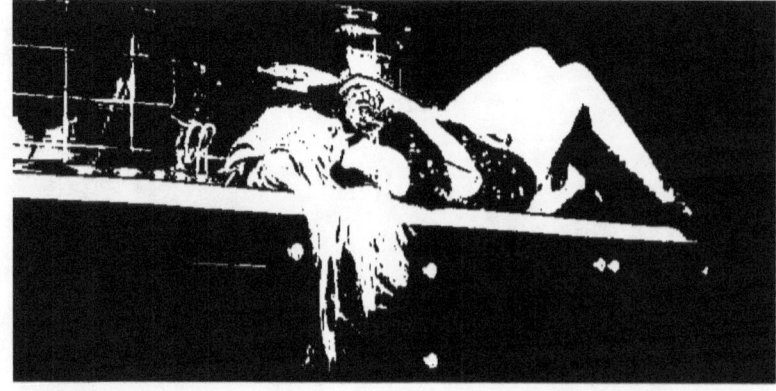

russian doll

Inside me, there is another me
diminished by shame.
Inside the other me, there is
a very small me
shrivelled by disgust.

winter

ft. j travis grundon

And that morning,
the embrace of
a new kind of cold:
pale, longing lips.

A vision of God
blinded by the light,
unmolested snow,
my last December.

hungover #2

They roll over,
heavy with disturbed sleep,
facing a clump of hair
on a long-abandoned pillow.
They scratch their bodies,
flakes of dismay
scatter the floor.
They look at their faces,
puffed up with alcohol
and hollow eyes swallowed
by the hopeless baring
of an interminable wait.
They throw away their mirrors,
not wanting to see
what they have become and
their soon-decaying skin
gnarled away by years of
fear and guilt.
They bury the memory of love
under cheap prints and disposable cloth.
They hug themselves tight
and recall all the good times
with people they never met,
people they will never see again,
ghosts of a life that has become
a distant, distorted dream
in a moldering world.
They couldn't stop destroying.

time to pretend

Mum says you can't go there,
but she never says why.
The minute she's off to have dinner out
and you have the evening to yourself,
you cake mascara and lipstick
over your little, young face.
You cross the threshold to
this weird, forbidden world.
The snarling man at the door
barely looks at your fake ID.

. . .

You bring the covers
over your cold body.
You don't like the taste in your mouth
or the memory of those hands.
You hear the key turn through the door
and smell Mum's perfume
and wish you'd listened,
and wish she'd told you,
and you know you can't turn back time,
so, you pretend to sleep
and pretend you are fine.

things i've seen and the things i think i've seen

Brown paper bag:
dead Labrador
abandoned by a curb.
People walking by,
not noticing,
and, in my head,
a funeral for a dog.

Old lamp post:
World War Two
unexploded bomb.
Trod on carelessly
by nearby school pupils,
and, in my head,
debris and mangled remains.

Forgotten coat on a branch:
Hanged man swinging
to non-existent wind,
by oblivious drivers
at a busy traffic light,
and, in my head,
prayers for a chimera.

little pain

It's always here,
nagging
like stitches
following surgery,
pulling at my skin.

It's always here,
dormant.

Flaring up,
catching my patched-up heart
with sly surprise.

I wrap it in a blanket,
keep it warm, pampered,
nestled against my chest,
feed it wine and tears.
That little pain
that is always a part of me.

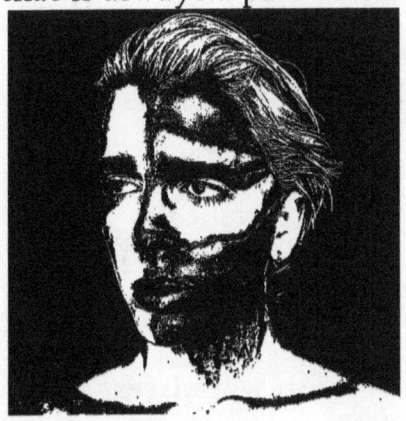

that fight we had brewing

We need to address
the elephant in the room.
That fat bastard
has been sucking out
all the oxygen,
leaving us gasping for breath
as we shatter those eggshells
fragments of anger
scattering around the place.
Your mother and mine,
that flirt from 2003,
my demanding boss,
your unsurprising
chicken surprise
all burn on the altar
of our frustrations
that smells of charred flesh
and too much cumin.
Later,
tired,
as the flames slowly die,
we make up,
wash the taste of
our bitter words

with wet kisses,
shed tears and clothing,

lick those fresh wounds,
finally reunified
under the watchful eye
of a fucking
pachyderm.

3am drunk text #3

I want

To kiss

Goodbye

The mouth

That never says

The words

I reserve for

Another

And leave

This insanity,

Prison

remembrance saturday

I lay dead, imaginary
flowers
on the grave of your
memory,
slowly trace
the stone-cold letters
of your tombstone
with a middle finger
that I will keep raised
a little while longer.
Just for you.

words

Falling down
a black hole,
bouncing
against sides
of a vacuum well,
and echoing
nothing,
sentences
forgotten,
distorted,
stretching
long and vain
into immaterial,
unintelligible
infinity.
Epitaph
hindsight,
a lifetime
of wrong turns,
and pleas
falling into
an already dug-up
void.

woman in mirror

Foundation too pale
for the dark cairns around
eyes that no longer shut.
Blusher too pink
for a complexion
drained of the rosiness
of joy and excitement.
Lipstick too bright
for an austere mouth
stingily hoarding
the last of the smiles.

little white lies

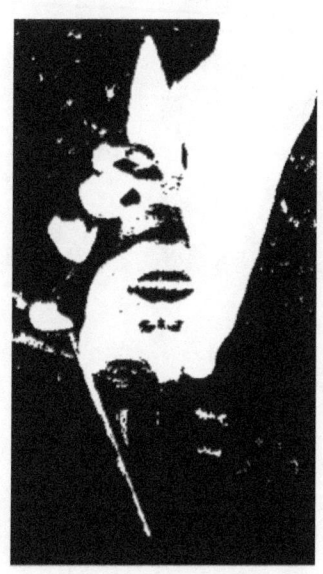

Sticky lip balm pout,
pointy pink tongue
licking tart dried-glue
running along the edge
of thick, glossy paper
sealing the destiny
of a message:
greetings and loving words
and those little white lies
easing the conscience
of one who never visits.

vanishing

She walked into the woods
on a starry night
and never
came out,

her footprints
quickly fading,
drowning into the mud,
soon overtaken by others.

Years on,
they found her.
Not her *really*—
the curled-up
bones of her:

long, white fingers
still clutching
prized possessions
of a lifetime.

A lighter
all out of flames

A rock
all out of bruises

And a picture
all out of faces.

tombstones

A life well-lived.
Acronyms were not her friends.
Great father, average husband.
A life well-lived?
John Something Something.
Finally.
Glug, glug.
She believed in iteration.
You ain't getting that back.
I regret nothing.
We buried you with your travel mug.
Name and message **TBC**.
Reunited with her daughter.
Pass the burgers, Jesus.
Evil man, thief of trees and innocence.
I demand a recount.
Cats!
Going to Hell, need anything?
I've taken all your secrets.
A life well-lived?
We will remember love.
Shipwreck.
Lived fast, died wet.
I told you so, Margaret.

A life.

wrestling the beast

It comes in at night,
insinuates itself into the room, smoke-like,
seeping through cracks and gaps.
When I notice its presence,
it's already too late,
and the fumes turn into
the acrid smell of sweat,
as it rests heavy on top of me,
spreads inside, covering my mouth,
turning my pleas into muffled whimpers.
...
My neck creaks from the strong headlock
and my teeth grind from
the memory of its salacious whispers,
its menacing murmurs,
threats of car accidents
and unrecognizable bodies
pulled out of carbonized tin cans,
unfortunate falls and incurable diseases,
phone calls announcing the unannouncable,
wrong turns into dark roads.
...
I try to wrestle it away from the children
and cling at its ethereal dress,
claw at its immateriality
as it slowly climbs up the stairs,
flashing that bright blade

before it slits little throats,
leaving me choosing
impossibly small coffins
over and over again,
as dawn rises and
the shadows of my insanity
shorten and slowly disappear.

wreckage

The wood whinges
before it cracks.
Water comes in fast.
Screams of terror
rise into the darkness.

She doesn't wait
for the boat to spill its entrails
into the inky sea,
or for them to crack her skull.

She jumps,
recoiling at the coldness,
and the horrifying abyss
beneath her.

She swims fast,
away from the wreck,
the rats, the screams,
and the two little voices
calling out for her.

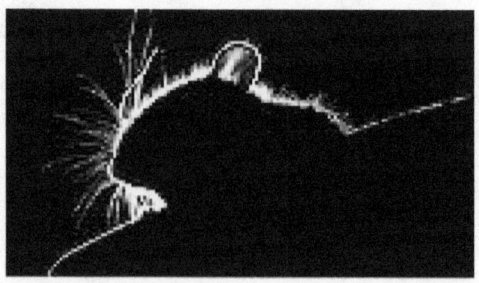

toxic

ft. stephen j golds

The cowardly smoke
of a weak yet never-ending
dumpster fire
raising slowly around me,
stinging my eyes and
choking my words with
millions of acrid
dust particles.
Here,
knowing
the only things
that celebrate the dead
are crowds and crows.
I sit, picking at myself
in moldy-green hallways of
broken mirrors and places
where smudged
plate-glass windows reflect
ghosts that will never leave.
They were never really here.

last words

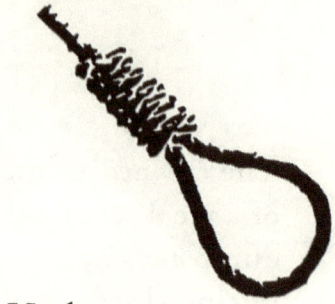

They ask,
as they fix the electrodes,
if he has any last words.

He keeps his head down,
his mouth shut.

I regret nothing.

Knuckles bruised from beatings,
blood pouring from stab wounds

Underwear
ripped from underaged girls.

I regret
nothing.

Screams,
gurgles,
pleas.

I regret
nothing.

He looks up
and shakes his head.

I regret

Nothing.

bedtime routine

I lie down
in a casket-like tub,
my pallid body
listless underwater.

I shave my legs
and run my palm
on smooth, warm limbs,
and remember
I will be
devoured by worms.

I brush my teeth,
I floss,
and spit death
all over the bathroom sink.

How much longer?

repetitive

ft. stephen j golds

It comes when the dreams don't, the midnight
walls constricting –
within the gut of Jonah's whale. A mind like
mosquito bites,
thoughts twisting like stagnant laundry or a
wonky child's windup toy.
Staring into a colorlessness with dry eyes.
Gnawing the night away with each wring of a
bloodied lip,
body twitching to the rhythm of
an invisible metronome.
It's here, always
casting its searing iron,
time after time, branding your soul
with the rusty-red glow
of inferno.

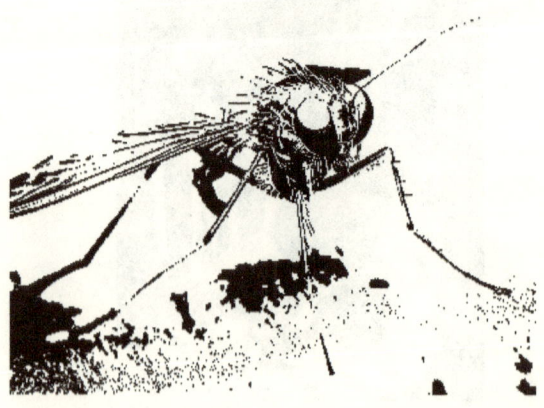

the only

sounds left

the only sounds left

I taste the bitterness
of the liquor,
feel it slowly crowding
my bloodstream,
my thoughts
gently wrapped in
cotton woo.
I pour another
and another,
the soft fabric tightening,
smothering
that untamed longing,
reducing it to nothing
but the hum of
an empty conversation,
and the footsteps
of a ghost
in a hollow chamber.

hide and seek

Down the cellar,
there's crying,
screaming echoed,
travelling up the stairs,
losing power
with every step,
and reaching them
in quiet, washed-down
moans and meows.
They stop and listen
for a moment,
eyebrows creased,
necks tilted.
They shake their heads,
raise their shoulders,
and get on with their
ordinary lives.

queen of hearts

She sits on a pile of
discarded bones,
rips the remaining
shreds of flesh
that she gnarls into pulp,
licks lips stained with blood,
sucks sticky, plump fingers,
rolls around and grinds
skeletons into dust,
lies back and waves her arms
up and down, bird of prey.
Opens and closes her legs
like she's done so many times,
luring them with promises of love.
Angel of death among
mounting carcasses.

trick or treat

I can't tell
if you love
or
use me.
All I know
is
I'm in your
dirty,
broken
thoughts.

sleepwalking

I'm tired of it all,
but I can't close my eyes

I go through the motions,
sipping,
spilling
unnecessary coffee
all over the feet
that no longer
need to wear shoes.

I go through the motions,
dropping,
throwing
the empty mug
on the kitchen floor
that I no longer
bother cleaning.

I roam my house
counter-clockwise,
hoping to bring back
joy
and happy memories.

the new her

He makes up words,
words she doesn't get,
doesn't like.
Words that describe
a new version of her
that he modelled
with cold, robotic hands
working spit and spite
into immobilizing clay.
Her mouth forever shut,
her eyes forever downcast.

He makes up words,
sculpts them with
the lacerating
edge of a knife
and throws them at her,
over and over until
she becomes them.

house of cards

My mind:
an arrow-shaped
sanctuary
sheltering wild dreams
and ambitions
one day toppled,
crumbling onto itself,
scattering onto the floor.
Slippery rectangles
sliding in all directions,
Aces lost
under the couch,
Joker stuck
under a dusty wardrobe
and the Queen of Hearts
forever gone.

the conversations in my head

Words seep
through my brain,
uninvited,
with the constant,
weak trickle
of a mall fountain
partially blocked
by an abandoned
fun-fair prize goldfish.

memento

She brings back fragments of him,
tastes them:
the tip of her finger
smacked against her mouth,
remembering
the tart grimace of his lips
as he uttered harsh words.

She listens to them once more,
slowly lifting her hands from her ears,
letting the dissonant truths
seep in with the
screeches of a bird of prey.

She unravels visions of a time
long gone, never forgotten:
old paper calendars
spitting smudged dates
of stolen times,
youth and carelessness
shredded to nothing
but mascara tears
on a torn pillow.

sang d'encre

Rusty fluid rushing
too quickly
through my limbs,
my head thumping,
the *thud, thud, thud*
of blood polluted
by too much anguish.

It's 2am.
Do you know
Where your children are?

Where are the
children?
"*Je me fais un sang*
d'encre,"
my mother used to say:
"My blood is
turning to ink."
And it does—I feel it
darkening with every
street corner,
dim underpath,
unlit road,
shallow ditch
that my brain navigates

Looking.
Looking.
Looking.
Where are the
children?

It's 3am.
Do you know
Where your children are?

The *thud, thud, thud*
of my ink-blood
pumping
in my ears,
the swooshing
sound of me drowning
in my own head

It's 4am.
I know
where my children are.
My children are
upstairs,
asleep.

It's 5am.

attempted ice queen

I wish my hurt
could glide over
the smooth back
of a frozen lake,

but I'm
melting
holes of
heart-stopping,
ice-cold water
under my hot-
blooded skin

and
drowning.

haiku for a disappointing man

Small steps leading me
further away from the sad
memory of you.

every time

Every time I look at you,
you die a little.
I run cold, weary fingers
through your graying hair,
cling to the warmth of you.
I lay my head on
your chest
and listen to the
quiet thud of your
aliveness.
I press my mouth
on your lips,
remembering
all the times that I didn't,
and vow
to glean
all the love
that we have left.

un-love

This poem was nominated for Best of The Net 2022.

We escape into the night,
where your lips meet mine
even though you don't like me
and I don't like you.
We try to fuck in a bush
even though it's a holly
and the ground is wet,
but I can't be bothered
and I enjoy your disappointment.
We rearrange our clothes
and we go back to the party
and I sip tepid beer
while scanning the room
for the next person
I will pretend to love.

summer evening

ft. david cranmer

A quiet evening with you, on the veranda,
light illuminating your golden hair.
You in that tube top and gazing down
smoldering flame. Smoldering out,
'til all that remained were dark skies
to keep company with memories of you.

A quiet evening with you, hot air waltzing,
stale look in your dirt-brown eyes.
And in your mouth, words you no longer mean.
The burning light of longing slowly
tarnished, a flicker growing ever fainter,
since that first morning, after.

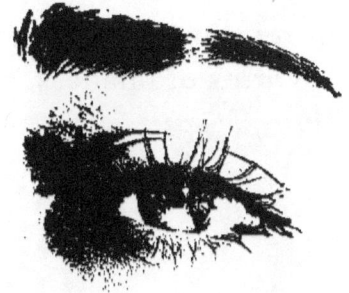

haikus to nowhere

I fall asleep in
my luggage packed for nowhere,
wake up unhappy.

Wake up exactly
in the same place as last year,
but with more wrinkles.

Fall asleep again
on the same page of the same
book of sad grudges.

Missed milestones, and missed
growing, aging family
opportunities.

Lost forever in
this vortex of idleness,
tedium, despair.

becoming bark

Outstretched arms
swaying,
waving her in

Gnarly fingers
rapacious,
rooting her in

molten scales
crawling up her
limbs,
conquering her body.

Among falling leaves,
she remains.

unanswered

They dig right under where it is,
where it should be,
where you point
a molten finger,
underneath
that stone angel.
This is where she is,
Was. Her eternal residence
below moody skies,
avalanches
of unanswered questions
rage,
tears.
They dig, but she's not there.
Revolving blue lights
revealing confusion,
panic,
consternation.
"She's gone," they say.
She's gone, you can see
a box empty
of all that was left.
Proof.
Reality.
Tragedy.
She's gone and with it,
the murmured claims
of your insanity.

And
you will never know.

Thanks for reading! Find more transgressive fiction (poems, novels, anthologies) at: Outcast-Press.com
Twitter & Instagram: @OutcastPress
Facebook.com/OutcastPress1

GoFund.Me/074605e9 (Outcast-Press: Short Story Collection)
Amazon, Kindle, Target, Barnes & Nobel

Email proof of your review to OutcastPressSubmissions@gmail.com & we'll mail you a free bookmark!

20 dark short stories by debut and veteran subversive writers like Craig Clevenger, Greg Levin, Lauren Sapala, Stephen J. Golds, Sebastian Vice, Paige Johnson, and more! Everything from serial killers and speculative cannibals to strippers and smack addicts.

more from outcast press

Paper lanterns and petty crime. Whiskey bars and beach confessions. One-night stands and childhoods that led to cheating, self-harm, and paranoia.

From OCD and grief to benign inspirations like antiseptic cream and call-waiting, Stephen J. Golds examines life with a sigh only sometimes wistful. Before an urban Japanese backdrop, we ride w/ him amid subway delays and panic attacks, careening cars and horror movies through 45 illustrated poems.

about the author

Twitter: @Fijo_Frenchie   Site: PunkNoirMagazine.com

BF Jones is French and lives in the U.K. with her husband, three kids, and two cats. She is co-editor of *Punk Noir Magazine* alongside Stephen J. Golds, fellow Outcast Press poet and noir novelist. Her other works include:

Artifice, 27 stories answering the question: What really happens behind closed doors?

Something Happened at 2a.m. (Anxiety Press, 2022), a collection of interconnected flash set in a small English suburb where a lot seems to happen in the dead of night.

5 Years, a David Bowie-inspired chapbook made in collaboration with Stephen J. Golds and David Cranmer.

Jones is currently working on a poetry book called *She* that follows an aging woman through her descent into madness, and a crime novella set in 1980s Corsica. The latter she is attempting to write in French, which she hasn't done in over a decade.

www.ingramcontent.com/pod-product-compliance
Lightning Source LLC
Chambersburg PA
CBHW030043100526
44590CB00011B/319